Glass Half Empty

PRECIOUS DEVINE CLAY

authorHOUSE®

AuthorHouse™
1663 Liberty Drive
Bloomington, IN 47403
www.authorhouse.com
Phone: 1 (800) 839-8640

Published by AuthorHouse 08/06/2018

ISBN: 978-1-5462-3855-3 (sc)
ISBN: 978-1-5462-3854-6 (e)

Library of Congress Control Number: 2018904875

Print information available on the last page.

Any people depicted in stock imagery provided by Getty Images are models, and such images are being used for illustrative purposes only. Certain stock imagery © Getty Images.

This book is printed on acid-free paper.

Because of the dynamic nature of the Internet, any web addresses or links contained in this book may have changed since publication and may no longer be valid. The views expressed in this work are solely those of the author and do not necessarily reflect the views of the publisher, and the publisher hereby disclaims any responsibility for them.

written with love

when i realized that revealing my truths made me *uncomfortable* i took a step out on faith and *did it anyway.*

Contents

Coming Clean

i have seen things but i avoided the truth
the signs were vivid to the naked eyes
no detail that stood out
i guess it just took time to figure you out
Passive i held my tongue
afraid of the things i would say
not because of it being
the wrong choice of words
but my fear of losing you
what had been the hardest
thing to say became truth
even without words.

love truly is self-sacrificing
so what are you willing to give

as writer 3 things you will do:
-ruffle a few feathers
-make some people uncomfortable
-touch the souls of the universe

when i cried i prayed you heard
wish i had eyes like an owl large enough to prey on
your smile
i had arms large enough to wrap you in
i guess my love wasn't strong enough to keep you
there

we walked together
there lie our footprints
your trail stopped
and there i walked alone

the world was created in such a way that man could not have created alone

i would always say the love i had for you was
strong i was willing to give everything
had you let me
then i would know

you were my soulmate
make no mistake our souls were compatible

do understand that love is a choice
and i chose to love you

we both said it was fate that we met
you didn't live in california somewhere
you lived close enough to home to destroy mine

7 billion people in the world you're the only one
who gave me life

your looks never truly mattered
i felt your spirit
that's when i witnessed true beauty

you were most relevant
because of me
it was my fault
i put you on
a pedestal
mainly because
i thought
you were
worth it
somehow seeing your worth
took away
from mine

your silence killed me in which i did not deserve
i extended my hand
for nothing in return
my cries were in silence
i wish you heard
i went to war with myself you handed me the sword

i did everything right so at least i thought i just
created an easy path for you to disappoint

any part of you that you offered i thought was
good enough
reality was i sold myself
short

all the things i have been through
you say i have not been
through much
the biggest torment was in my head
forgive me for i have held back
you could not see
so that made me much less than you
my biggest battle was within
i apologize for i have held back
my pain was not meant for you.

i have taken pain away
and i have caused it.

you signed me in as i stood by your side
always aware of my surroundings but i felt safe
enough to walk off
hearing other children around that caught my
attention
not long before i could turn around
you took off
i ran for you but turned away.
                    -where'd you go

down those stairs lived hell
one by one i went down
to return & tell a lie
the look in her eyes brought so much fear
i couldn't help but tell a lie
spent several weeks at a time in an office
speechless being asked questions
that had no truth
taking wooden pieces out of a box
building them to the top
just so they can fall
eventually i gained the courage to tell it all

she'd never be enough
you were only being half loved
i do apologize for calling that love
lusting only your soul
i had much to give
but you only took what was needed
she'd never be enough, so i guess were
even

i was broken you didn't stay
truth is…
it wasn't worth it anyway

i could remember growing up i would look in the
mirror staring at myself
my grandmother would come over visit
as i continue to glance somehow, she witnessed
she told me to stop staring at myself because i was
beautiful for a long time i couldn't accept myself
because i thought i made others uncomfortable
my comfort should have come from within
oh, grandmother i wish i could have seen what your
eyes viewed
in the mirror i only seen a reflection of confusion
but when you left me it seems the love
i should have had for myself got strong
i see i was more resilient than i thought.

i starved myself knowing i was hungry
afraid to eat knowing I would be bullied
the real damage was being done at home
when i would binge eat for days upon weeks
gaining excessive weight, the only outlet
i had was to write let the doctors tell
it that was becoming unhealthy
it landed me in place i never expected to be
strapped me down on a stretcher
as if i was a threat to others
they were so excited to have me as the new girl
and i was just happy to be accepted for
once i was confined in a room full of girls
but we all had so much in common
i was placed in the hot seat being forced to
open get the help i so desperately needed

i would bleed for months at a time i
was unsure on how i was surviving
shoe strings being taken from my
shoes to not be of self-harm
being placed on a strict diet
only able to leave the floors if my
conduct was in the clear
taking anti -depressants to control the depression
having to poke my fingers every day
and i wasn't even a diabetic
craving for that snickers bar
knowing i could not have it
eating teddy grams every night
to stop the cravings
consoling other girls to stop
them from misbehaving
one thing i was sure of i wasn't alone.

i waited for your truth
i knew one day it would come
i waited an entire year to finally profess my love
you asked me how i felt
i can breathe now
praying in my head
you wouldn't leave
i had never been so afraid
to lose someone who was only temporary.

you say you want to be a fool for the one you love
well i hate to be the barer of bad news
it doesn't mean much if the feeling is not mutual
we sit and make excuses for why we fall in love with
hope
hopes that they will love us back
maybe hopes that you will someday get them to
change
that those hopes will someday become truth
we blind ourselves with manipulation &lies
that package built at the devils' hands
we believe the lies they tell are shielding our hearts
what we don't realize its creating self- destruction
we allow them to come in and out so freely
without guarding ourselves

she died to want you
she died to need you
she died to love you
she died to breathe you
she died to hold you
she died to see you
she died to speak
but you failed to listen

i never knew i could love like this
meeting you was the best thing
abandonment was the furthest thing
regret doesn't live in me so i refuse

Broken Letters

the length of her hair
you could wrap yourself in
an island you could spend your life on
a smile that could light up your soul

everything inside of me isn't fighting fair
the things that have attacked me
didn't attack the women in me
it attacked the little girl

which is perfectly
normal.

contemplating on so
many ways to change
you want the change
but unsure of how to
get it
after so many doubts
and fears
you began to figure
it out
and the goal becomes
bigger than the doubt
you start to put things
into perspective
to become better
you speak aloud
because your excited
and you want others to
be excited for you

you leave your heart
open enough for
disappointment with
those high expectation
that maybe they'll care
you learn to take the
good with the bad
every time you think
you've come up with a
solution
another problem arises
now you just find
another solution to a
different problem
this cycle then becomes
infinite
so, stop telling your
dreams to the devil
and better yourself for
the better.

i fell short on how to fully love myself
most of the time we all lose sight of that
i was so in tune with giving love to someone else
and i forget about self
no matter how much i tried loving
i always fell short of being worthy
i could never understand why love would never
take a chance on me
because when you're this self-less even one the
best things in life don't seem free
i cared less about myself
to focus on everyone else's needs
no matter how much you give to the world
the key is to not always expect that back in return

as you give yourself with open arms with no
stipulations
you set the cycle on how others will treat you
those you love unconditionally who had no
intentions on loving you in the first place
i always told myself that I would never regret things
in my life
because sometimes life it can be just that full of
regrets
things like that for most people seem to be a bit
mediocre or taken for granted
for someone like myself i'd cherish each moment
because time you can't get it back
you can't fast-forward
you can't press pause
you can only live in each moment
you stayed around long enough for me to express
how much I truly loved you
Your happiness was always first
Near or far you'll always have a home in my heart.

you were ashamed of me
the best way to show me was to keep your distance
i died on the inside from feeling unworthy
i questioned things that my instincts already had
the answers to
what i really needed was the answers from you
how i tried to keep my heart shielded from feeling
pain
Somehow the love i had in my heart for you over
powered everything
i was good enough for words
even that wasn't enough
i came with no warnings
although i came guarded
i somehow lost my armor
your smile gave me hope
for I have felt a many hopeless moments
your presence gave me satisfaction
i know i was strong on my own
it felt good to fell wanted in some sort of way
i believe because i wasn't fully in love with self
i accepted only what i though was good enough
for that i am ashamed

wishing i could have spoken my last words
i was given no choice but to only let go.

with pain you can create
something beautiful

you couldn't break my heart but you can taunt my
emotions
even cause me some destruction

i found myself at the heels of your feet
i don't owe you anything

how do you see beauty in a mad man...?
she's a woman

i have begged for mercy at your feet
continuous wondering thoughts
i sought out for love
i thought love is supposed to prevail
for the home i have built for it
no one lives there

no matter how in depth my words are
not much is needed to be said
the less i speak the louder my thoughts become
the more i listen the bigger my eyes are
-*focused*

one thing im sure of about love is that it can be
scary
that's when most people run because they have
not been loved properly

you brought my spirit peace
you gave me hope
thank you for the security

she is beauty nothing short thereof

when the wind whistles somehow
it sings your name
my ears began to dance

now i know what you think of me you
tell me every time we argue

i loved you but i was told how to feel
it was said to be infatuation but i
am aware of the difference
i loved you, so you're unable to tell me otherwise,
if so you can speak it to my heart

i do a lot of thinking during the day
i wondered what our conversations
would be like if we still spoke
just daydreaming with hope

all these years ive blamed myself for rejection
all the things i have subjected myself to
only left the door open for others to disrespect me
i wore my heart on my sleeve instead of pity
i continued to believe in love although
love continued to deceive me
i still loved love although love doesn't love me

i thought i had to fix myself to be loved
always walking in the shadow
of a good girl

i wasn't perfect by any means
nor have i ever portrayed myself to be
i figured if i did most things right love would find
its way to me

it somehow makes you wonder of why you waited
in the first place

for every door i opened
there was a closed one

we all have the perception that
love is supposed to hurt
when it's just the opposite
all the worlds pains are confused with love
when love has no pains
love knows no boundaries
love always wins

she grew tired of herself, so she
thought loving someone else
would fill that void
when the two of you together
formed a place called
hell
trying to build a home

i knew when i first picked up a pen my mind
would create a storm that would never end

she's so selfish with her heart
no one deserves it except the one that doesn't

i apologized for everything that wasn't anything
-learn to be unapologetic

when asked whats is my worth
i had no response
my tongue became paralyzed
from there my search
began

i felt loving and caring was my obligation to you
listening to your chosen
words of unworthy good for nothing
views of me
i have done nothing but try to prove
i was spectacular enough

One piece

you came here to take your anger
and hostility out upon me
when its you whom continue to
make misery your first
priority

you've heard my pain in my tone
you've listened to my cries
you've spoken until you were
blue in the face
still i heard not one word
you've loved me unconditionally with
physically no face to a name
with uncensored reality you seen me

i cried telling myself its okay to be angry
to talk about the things and people that hurt me
how cold-chilling this world could be
it knows no sympathy
empathy
it shows no remorse
the longer i sat and waited for it
the more it began to disappoint

i sure i needed a change so i cut my hair
i needed to feel brand new
but that only came from within
i needed to be stronger
i tried to change other people around me
but neglected to change myself

you can never deny me we are identical

before there was anyone there was me and you
-my brother

one of the most daunting things in the world
is trying to see the good in everyone

we're like crabs on a rock waiting for high tides

i have become so isolated no tourist can find me

i am tired of trying to make you see me
doing such is impossible
how aren't you able to see me with open eyes
your eyes are sewn shut
i am gold

you've complimented me more than she ever has

when a woman is this good how do you live with
knowing she slipped through your fingers

the cowardice in you helps me to understand
why you never gave me the closure i needed

as the year went by in all of your successes
i still gave standing novation
how i was forced to applaud you in silence
because to you i didn't exist anymore
how i was only a shoulder when
no one else desired you

once upon a time you seen me or
maybe it was camouflage
trying to blend in
when you are really less than what you show

when asked what is seen
there is hesitation
looking down when speaking
when looking into the eyes of
others became intimidating
seeking out validation because of uncertainty
certain she didn't love her enough to be so sure
shattered face but appears to be so put together
ran away from mirrors because of the reflection
abstained from wanting to give
myself she was so pure
mascara dripped from the crevices of her eyes
onto her matted lips of smudged lipstick
she tried to disguise her natural beauty
because the true her was an unknown beast

my mirrors have told me so many lies
it eventually shattered

i have learned to bow without an audience

if i am angry enough my hands will turn into flames

perhaps one of the most painful things i
have ever felt was being in love alone

i was confused on which way to turn
there were so many mixed signals

i tell you that im okay because
im good at hiding pain

we create our own misery with
to many expectations

it was so dark the devil became hungry for a soul

small enough to sting like gunfire

i did not want to be high like the clouds
i wanted to be higher than them.

once upon a time i was a dark
hole inside of a dark hole

every moment spent with you felt like a vacation

never become addicted to being a
victim for you will always remain one

if you dig deep enough you'll
discover imperfections

my world was a fairytale until i awakened

you suppress pain long enough it will eventually roll
over and create its own storm

i did not feel accepted until i
started accepting myself

i am always in the ring alone

when someone says they know you
ask them what they think they know
they will begin to name things
what they are naming is not who you are
but the perception they have of you

she cut her hair because she thought
it would make her feel free
lately she has seen herself frown
more than she smiles
she raised the question of how to
feel the void of loneliness
you miss those people that were in your
life you wish were still existent although
their alive well and breathing
you try to drown yourself in your dreams goals and
aspirations but yet it still feels something is missing
she cries because she has created these
illusions of happiness in her mind that
maybe someday love would reveal itself.
she no longer wants to compete with one
of the many things in life that are free.
she has seen the different sides the many
different ways love could be so two-faced.

no one wants to be responsible
for breaking my heart

i have been placed on reserve without notification

Printed in the United States
By Bookmasters